To the victims of Hurricane Katrina

Contents

Introduction by Katrina vanden Heuvel | xi

Dictionary of Republicanisms | 1

Acknowledgments | 157

Postscript | 163

List of Cartoons

Clean by Ellen Weinstein | 18

Freedom March by Peter Kuper | 46

God by Joe Ciadiello | 51

Honesty by Peter Kuper | 61

Ownership Society by Tim O'Brien | 98

Philosophy by Victor Juhasz | 105

Slave by Frances Jetter | 124

Ten Commandments by Barry Blitt | 132

Wal-Mart by Sam Weber | 143

Wolfoleon by Steve Brodner | 148

Introduction

THE THREAT

George W. Bush, a self-proclaimed straight-talking Texan, has been roundly lampooned for his weak grasp of the English language: "subliminable," "resignate," and "transformationed" being only a very few of his malapropisms. But as ridiculous as Bush sometimes sounds, it would be shortsighted to misunderestimate the president or the right-wingers who put him in power, because they deliberately and consciously *never* say what they mean or mean what they say.

Over the past few decades, the radical Right has

engaged in a well-funded, self-conscious program of Orwellian doublespeak, transforming the American political discourse to suit their political ends. Think tanks like the Cato Institute routinely market phrases for their political resonance, like personal vs. private accounts. Frank Luntz, the Republican pollster, lexicographer, and MSNBC regular who combines Madison Avenue techniques with K Street connections, sends out regular missives informing Republican operatives and politicians on how to spin conservative policy proposals. (He was recently on *The Daily Show* demonstrating his talents, defining "manipulation" as "explanation and education.") Paul Wolfowitz admitted to *Vanity Fair* that Weapons of Mass Destruction was agreed upon as the reason to go to war with Iraq because it was the most sellable. And we all know how that turned out.

Theirs is the Mary Poppins strategy: a little bit of sugar makes the medicine go down. And the medicine has been very bad indeed. Under George W. Bush, the deficit reached its highest level in our history: $412 billion with a total debt figure of $7,768,431,198,132 (that's seven—almost eight— *trillion* dollars) that climbs, on average, by over a billion a day. The dollar is in free fall. Gas prices have shot through the roof. Job creation is at a post–World War II low in America. (Conversely, job creation in India and China has been progressing at a wonderful rate.) The tepid economic recovery has stalled. The number of uninsured is at a record high, as the cost of health insurance rises at double digits year after year. The country is bitterly divided. The rest of the world loathes us. Afghanistan is once again the world's leading exporter of heroin (the War on Terror is apparently at cross-purposes with the War on Drugs). The Iraq invasion, which was supposed to be a cakewalk, has turned into a quagmire, and the elections failed to slow insurgency attacks. The

American military is stretched to the breaking point as the casualty rate rises and the enlistment rate falls. The Abu Ghraib torture photos are being used by al Qaeda as recruitment posters. The list goes on and on and on.

The world's richest and most powerful nation is being run into the ground by the man whose business associates nicknamed Arbusto, after his failed oil company. This anti-Midas—everything golden he touches turns to lead—has taken us for a ride down the garden path, at exactly the same historical moment that China and India are rising. History hasn't ended, but the American Century may have. Our security is threatened, our reputation is in tatters, our economy tips precariously on a house of dollars foreign banks no longer want. Things are only going to get worse if something isn't done, and soon.

We can no longer hope the Republicans will turn the ship of state around before we hit the iceberg.

Bush, Cheney, DeLay, Rumsfeld, Rove, et al., were more interested in saving Terri Schiavo than the country. Those of us riding in steerage have a stark choice to make: We can either abandon ship, or wrest control of the wheel from a captain and crew who are too blinkered to see the danger ahead.

Certainly the lifeboats are tempting. After the 2004 election, some compassionate Canadians set up a Web site, offering to sacrifice their single-hood to marry progressives who wanted to flee north. (As the *New Yorker's* Hendrik Hertzberg says, Canada makes us proud to be North Americans.) The number of Chinese-American graduate students who have returned to mainland China looking for job opportunities has risen dramatically. And ask any pregnant woman who has lived in both Europe and America where she'd rather have her baby, and you'll discover one of the reasons why America is no longer the de facto destination of choice for immigrants.

But however bleak the near future looks, we have no choice as patriots but to stay and fight. America's great gift to the world has been to promise, and then prove, that the future can always be better than the past. We have faced tough times and bad leaders (Nixon and the Vietnam era come to mind), and we will also weather these recent right-wing assaults on the principles of fundamental fairness that make this country great. Yes, we will stay and fight to retake our country from the forces of extremism, corruption, and incompetence that have set up shop in the White House, Capitol Hill, and K Street.

But to win this battle, we need to think beyond the electoral. This is not simply a matter of flipping a few seats in Congress or electing a Democrat president in 2008. This is a battle over what ideas, values, and principles should animate the life of our nation. The radical Right's assault on the liberal consensus did not begin with Bush, nor will it end with him. He is but the most recent in a line that stretches from Goldwater to Reagan to Gingrich, the most recent embodiment of a political ideology that seeks to end the government's role in redressing the vast inequalities created by what Pope John Paul II called "unbridled, savage capitalism." Their agenda pads the wallets of the wealthy and punishes the poor, and threatens to turn America into Latin America, a nation of haves and have-nots, a nation without safety nets, a nation without a middle class, a nation without peace and without allies.

Before we can win this great battle of ideas, we must first debunk their political discourse, a veritable Orwellian code of encrypted language that twists common usage to deceive the public for the Republicans' own purposes. The key to their linguistic strategy is to use words that sound moderate to us but mean something completely different to them. Their tactics range from the childish use of antonyms ("clean" = "dirty") to the pseudo-academic use of prefixes ("neo" is a favorite) to the pernicious and very expensive rebranding of traditional political labels ("liberal") as an insult.

We need to break the code by building a Republican dictionary. Skewer their deceptions with the fine-tipped sword of satire. Lies melt away in the face of mockery. Laughter truly is the best medicine.

Here's an example of how it works:

THE METHOD

In Bush's 2005 State of the Union address, he mentioned "personal accounts" seven times but "private accounts" zero times, which is interesting because only a few months prior to that, he had been using both terms interchangeably. This was no mistake. The Republicans tested the phrase "private accounts" and found that public support was much lower than when the same, exact, identical concept was called "personal accounts." (Personally, I like "caring accounts," but they didn't ask me.)

So the White House and its paid spin doctors, many of whom play journalists on TV, took to the airwaves to push the phrase "personal accounts" and chastise anyone in the media who employs the banished words to characterize the administration's Social Security agenda. Proof positive, if more was needed, that language is power and debates are won or lost based on definitions.

But here is the really funny thing about Bush's first scheme for personal/private accounts, which for the moment are off the table but are likely to return. Not only are they not personal accounts, they're not private accounts either. They are, in fact, U.S. government loans. (Bear with me now, because this will only hurt for a moment.) You see, your payroll taxes will still be used to cover the benefits of current retirees, but under Bush's scheme the government will place a certain "diverted" amount into an account in your name. It sounds like a personal retirement account, but it's not: it's a loan. Because if your account does really well (above 3 percent), when you retire the government will deduct the money it lent you (plus 3 percent interest) from your monthly Social Security check, leaving you with almost the same amount you would have received under the current system. If your account does really poorly (below 3 percent), you are out of luck. According to the Congressional Budget Office, the expected average return will be 3.4 percent, so the net gain will be zero after management fees are deducted. So, who wins? Wall Street, not you.

But wait, it gets better. These personal accounts aren't exactly U.S. government loans either, because our government, under the fiscal stewardship of George W. Bush, is no longer running a surplus and therefore does not have the $3 trillion or so needed to cover the transition costs, and Bush refuses to raise taxes on his base (BUSH'S BASE, *n.* The wealthy).

So our government will have to borrow that cash. And if the last three years are any guide, our largest single loan officer will likely be the Central Bank of China. And who runs not only China's Central Bank, but also China itself and the Chinese people, with an iron fist? Why, it's our old friends, the democracy-loving, freedom-marching Chinese Communist Party. So Bush's personal retirement accounts = private retirement accounts = U.S. government loans = U.S. government borrowing = Chinese government lending = Chinese Communist Party loans.

Or, as we like to say in *The Dictionary of Republicanisms* land:

personal retirement accounts, *n.*

Chinese Communist Party loans.

THE RESPONSE

Unlike Republicans who rely on rich old cranks and intellectuals-for-hire to do their dirty work, we opened up the process to the people. For six months, thenation.com accepted suggestions from everyone who wanted to participate. The result was an overwhelming grassroots groundswell of hilarious submissions from citizens who are mad as hell and aren't going to take it anymore. Thousands of definitions were entered from all over the country, forty-four states in all, along with Puerto Rico and Washington, D.C. (We even received a few from outraged Canadians, Australians, and Brits.)

As would be expected, the blue states predominated, especially New York, Massachusetts, and California. But there were some surprises. The state with the most submissions was Texas, which only goes to show that no prophet is honored in his hometown. We also had strong showings from Tennessee, Georgia, and Kansas.

As momentum for the project grew, friends and allies joined the effort. TomDispatch.com asked its readers and writers to submit their own definitions. Reviewing the submissions from our Web site, certain trends became apparent. "Compassionate Conservative" and "Ownership Society" were the most popular targets. "No Child Left Behind" was the most common riff. The disaster in Iraq was the subject of the most outrage.

I have culled all of these submissions for the funniest, sharpest, most hard-hitting definitions. The best have been collected in this book. I hope they inspire you to action, to take back this great nation from those who are doing it such harm.

—Katrina vanden Heuvel
New York, 2005

abstinence-only sex education, *n.*

Ignorance-only sex education [Wayne Martorelli, Lawrenceville, NJ].

abuse, *n.*

Modern word for what was once referred to as torture. An interim term, soon to be replaced by "tough love" (which, in turn, is expected to be replaced by "freedom's caress") [Nick Turse, New York, NY].

accountability, *n.*

1. Never having to say you're sorry [Norm Conrad, Seattle, WA].

2. Buck? What buck? [Martin Richard, Belgrade, MT].

3. The deficit started under Clinton [Jeff Reitzes, Pleasant Hill, CA].

activist judge, *n.*

1. A judge who actively judges in a manner inconsistent with conservative ideology [Vanessa deKonick, Davis, CA].

2. One who makes fair and balanced decisions [Michael Haney, Napa, CA].

3. A judge who interprets the law as it is written [Kerry Jones, Houston, TX].

4. A judge who attempts to protect the rights of minorities, especially homosexuals, against the tyranny of the majority [Dan McWilliams, Santa Barbara, CA].

airport security, *n.*

1. Free feel-up [Sonja Woodward, San Jose, CA].

2. Method for citizens to prove their patriotism through the removal of shoes, belts, and push-up bras [Casey Pavelka, Poland, OH].

Alan Greenspan, *n.*

Former Randian fiscal conservative [Kenneth McGinis, New York, NY].

alarmist, *n.*

Any respected scientist who understands the threat of global warming [Dan McWilliams, Santa Barbara, CA].

ally, *n.*

Client state [Dave Graham, Carol Stream, IL].

alternative energy sources, *n.*

New locations to drill for gas and oil [Peter Scholz, Fort Collins, CO].

American idle, *n.*

A president who spends half his time on vacation, goes to bed early every night, and brags about not reading newspapers [Yvonne Julian-Hargrove, Fairfield, CA].

anti-Semite, *n.*

Anyone who disagrees with any aspect of Israel's political policy. Such individuals of Jewish heritage are more accurately defined as self-hating Jews [Christofer Nigro, Buffalo, NY].

axis of evil, *n.*

Cheney, Rove, and Rumsfeld [Sonja Woodward, San Jose, CA].

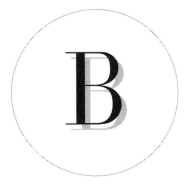

baby tax, *n.*

The $25,000 in national debt dumped on every newborn baby [Jim Woodbrey, Green Valley, AZ].

balanced, *adj.*

A lie that is given equal weight to the truth [Dorothy Chase, Montreal, QC, Canada].

bankruptcy, *n.*

A punishable crime when committed by poor people but not corporations [Beth Thielen, Studio City, CA].

bankruptcy bill, *n.*

The Pro-Usury Bill [Dave Argail, Nashua, NH].

big government, *n.*

1. Social Security.

2. Medicare.

3. Environmental protections.

4. Pell grants [Justin Rezzonico, Keene, NH].

Bill of Rights, *n.*

1. Archaic document purported to state actual rights of all citizens; not currently used [James Kerwin, CA].

bioconservatives, *n.*

Bush dynasty [Greg Filipek, Garden Grove, CA].

bipartisanship, *n.*

1. When conservative Republicans work with moderate Republicans to pass legislation that Democrats hate [Katrina vanden Heuvel, New York, NY].

2. When Democrats realize they don't have enough votes to stop anything and give up [Brant Lamb, Dexter, MI].

3. Another name for date rape [Grover Norquist, Third Level, Hell].

blue state, *n.*

The state of mind associated with Democrats and liberals after the 2004 election [Robert Reiley, New Orleans, LA].

"burning Bush," *n.*

A biblical allusion to the response of the President of the United States when asked a question by a journalist who has not been paid to inquire [Bill Moyers, New York, NY].

Bush-bending, *n.*

The distortion of facts by the Bush White House, particularly effective on mainstream journalists worried about access [Susan Carr, Tucson, AZ].

Bushit, *n.*

The words coming out of George W. Bush's mouth [Michael Fjeldstad, Brentwood, CA].

cakewalk, *n.*

1. Baghdad Airport Road [Jon Rudd, Bethesda, MD].

2. Taking the Hummer out for a scenic drive through a gauntlet of improvised explosive devices [Robert Clawson, Acton, MA].

carrot and stick, *phr.*

The rich get the carrot; the poor get the stick [Jonathan Friedman, Arecibo, PR].

catastrophic success, *n.*

1. Florida, 2000.

2. Ohio, 2004.

3. Tends to correspond to elections run by Republican election commissioners [Jacob McCullar, Austin, TX].

checks and balances, *n.*

1. What Bush is good at writing, and what he is good at making appear in red ink [Jacob McCullar, Austin, TX].

2. The system whereby the campaign checks of the few balance the interests of the many [Stephen R. Shalom, NJ].

cheese-eating surrender monkeys, *n.*

Citizens of a nation that supplied an army of eight thousand troops and a fleet of thirty-two battleships to support George Washington's victory at Yorktown, thereby securing American independence [Jon Rudd, Bethesda, MD].

chickenhawk, *n.*

A perspicacious bird of prey with an aversion to having its feathers ruffled; when the winds of war blow its way, it prefers to remain roosted and use its talons to feather its own nest [George Kontos, Bolinbrook, IL].

China, *n.*

See WAL-MART [Rebecca Solnit, San Francisco, CA].

clarify, *v.*

To repeat the same lie over and over again [Katrina vanden Heuvel, New York, NY].

class warfare, *n.*

1. Any attempt to raise the minimum wage.

2. Any attempt to limit the concentration of wealth in the hands of fewer and fewer plutocrats [Don Zweir, Grayslake, IL].

3. Any attempt to provide affordable health care for the working poor. [Ann Wegher, Montello, WI].

clean, *n.*

The word used to modify any aspect of the environment that Republican legislation allows corporations to pollute, poison, or destroy [Matthew Polly, Topeka, KS].

Clean Air Act, n.

A law that protects citizens from the hazards of breathing clean air [Justin Kodner, Princeton Junction, NJ].

clear skies, *n.*

1. Quality of atmosphere in which one can clearly see the air pollutants [Raymond Anderson, Rantoul, IL].

2. Excellent conduit for acid rain [Ron Russell, address unknown].

climate change, *n.*

1. The blessed day when the blue states are swallowed by the oceans [Ann Klopp, Princeton, NJ].

2. Euphemism for global warming, without the annoying implication that some regulations on corporations are required to stop it [Megan Ellis, Bellingham, WA].

common sense, *n.*

1. Modifier used for extreme, right-wing justices Bush wants to appoint to the courts [Steve Clark, Beach Park, IL].

2. The value Republicans like to ascribe to the American public to argue for positions that are unpopular. [Anon].

compassionate conservatism, *n.*

1. Thou shalt exploit thy neighbor for thyself [Peter Nightingale, Kingston, RI].

2. Poignant concern for the very wealthy [Lawrence Sandek, Twin Peaks, CA].

3. The inverse relationship between wealth and poverty: The greater the conservation of wealth in the hands of the few, the more poor there are for conservatives to feel compassion for [Gretchen Hecht, San Francisco, CA].

4. Republican preelection concern for the disadvantaged [Gary Hunter, Thomasville, NC].

5. (a). I got mine; (b). I got yours, too [Brian Kenner, Tervuren, Belgium].

6. A kinder, gentler McCarthyism [Robert Fuld, Unionville, CT].

7. A Subaru with a gun rack; *see* OXY-MORON [Tony Gouchie, Amherst, NS, Canada].

conviction, *n.*

Making decisions before getting the facts and refusing to change your mind afterwards [Paul Ruschmann, Canton, MI].

creationism, *n.*

1. Theory holding that humans are descended from mud, rather than apes [Robert Clark, Denver, CO].

2. Metaphysical belief that Republicans were created by God, while Democrats evolved from monkeys [Mike Brush, Boise, ID].

3. Pseudoscience that claims George W. Bush's resemblance to a chimpanzee is totally coincidental [Brian Sweeney, Providence, RI].

4. Science fiction [Stephen F. Cohen, New York, NY].

crusade, *n.*

1. Christian Jihad [McAlister Clabaugh, Washington, D.C.].

2. Slip of the tongue, meant to say "holy war" [Mike Tuson, Arlington, VA].

culture of life, *n.*

1. One where stem cells are pardoned, but not adolescents or the mentally handicapped on Death Row [Tod Mohebi, Pleasanton, CA].

2. One where only a zygote, embryo, or fetus deserves rights and protections, all of which are immediately withdrawn upon birth [Janet Daly, Hunts Point, WA].

3. Strange belief that Jesus felt more strongly about contraception and abortion than the death penalty of which he was a reluctant participant [Matthew Polly, Topeka, KS].

cut-and-run Republicans, *n.*

1. Cut taxes for special interests; run up deficits for our children.

2. Cut deals for contributors; run misleading campaigns.

3. Cut programs for the poor; run from the responsibility of government [Steve Kane, Thousand Oaks, CA].

Darwinism, *n.*

1. An unproven pseudoscientific theory, one of many, about the origin of species.

2. A proven social scientific fact about the moral superiority of the wealthy [Gary Schroller, Bellaire, TX].

death tax, *n.*

1. Estate tax [Shannon Wagner, Brooklyn, NY].

2. Tax intended to prevent the rich from creating a permanent aristocracy of wealth in this country [Dan McWilliams, Santa Barbara, CA].

deficit, *n.*

1. Something Reagan proved didn't matter [Dick Cheney, Unknown Location, USA].

2. Result of Republican "cut taxes and spend" fiscal discipline [Michael Fisher, Monte Rio, CA].

delay, *v.*

1. To put off facing the consequences of your unethical actions (*see* DeLAY, TOM) [George Davis, Blacksburg, VA].

DeLay, Tom, *n.*

1. Past tense of De Lie. [Rick Rodstrom, Los Angeles, CA].

2. Patronage saint [Andrew Magni, Nonatum, MA].

democracy, *n.*

1. Government of the corporations, by the corporations, for the corporations [Kevin Crifo, New York, NY].

2. My way or the highway [Daniel Quinn, London, England].

3. A country where the newspapers are pro-American [Michael Schwartz, address unknown].

4. A product so extensively exported that the domestic supply is depleted.

5. When they vote for us; *see* TYRANNY: When they vote for someone else [Rebecca Solnit, San Francisco, CA].

democratic ally, *n.*

The Emir of Kuwait, General Musharraf, the House of Saud, the King of Jordan, Vladimir Putin, Hosni Mubarak, etc. [Matthew Polly, Topeka, KS].

Democratic Leadership Council, *n.*

1. Complicit conservatism [Katrina vanden Heuvel, New York, NY].

2. Compassionate compliers [Lawrence Sandek, Twin Peaks, CA].

detainee, *n.*

Hostage without a ransom note [Raymond Anderson, Rantoul, IL].

detainment center, *n.*

Cuba; used by both Castro and Bush [Anon].

Dick Cheney, *n.*

The greater of two evils [Jacob McCullar, Austin, TX].

diplomacy, *n.*

1. Carry a big bomb.

2. Talk loudly until stick proves insufficiently big, then ask for help [Joy Losee, Gainesville, GA].

disengagement, *n.*

Bush's brain and his mouth [Sonja Woodward, San Jose, CA].

disgust, *n.*

The feeling Americans have for their political process and what passes for political dialogue. Rhymes with "discussed" [John Krogman, Albuquerque, NM].

dittohead, *n.*

An Oxy(contin)moron [Zydeco Boudreaux, Gretna, LA].

economic progress, *n.*

1. Recession.

2. Rising unemployment.

3. Minimum-wage freeze [Terry McGarry, Rockaway, NY].

4. When three out of five software engineers whose jobs were outsourced to India are able to find work as cashiers at Wal-Mart [Rob Hotman, Houston, TX].

election fraud, *n.*

Counting every vote [Dan McWilliams, Santa Barbara, CA].

elitists, *n.*

Everyone who has NPR programmed into their car-radio presets [Carter Turner, Blacksburg, VA].

embedded, *adj.*

In bed with [Lawrence Sandek, Twin Peaks, CA].

ending tyranny, *catchphr.*

1. Bombing followed by military occupation [Kerry Jones, Houston, TX].

2. Both shockingly and awesomely ineffective [Matthew Polly, Topeka, KS].

energy independence, *n.*

1. The Yucca Mountain renovation program [Kimberly Ellenberger, Beloit, WI].

2. The Caribou witness relocation program [Justin Rezzonico, Keene, OH].

English, *n.*

Language required to be spoken by immigrants applying for citizenship, but not a requirement for the president of the United States [Joy Losee, Gainesville, GA].

Environmental Protection Agency, *n.*

Economic Predators, Inc. [Arlie Hochschild, Berkeley, CA].

enlightened labor practice, *n.*

High salaries and lucrative options for CEOs, balanced by low salaries for ordinary workers [Michael Thomas, Socorro, NM].

entrepreneur, *n.*

Campaign donor [Michael Barry, West Medford, MA].

E.P.A., *acronym.*

Empower Polluters Agency. [Mary Ellen Reynolds, Tucson, AZ].

ethics committee, *oxymoron.*

Hibernating carnivore that only hunts when Democrats control the White House [Raymond Anderson, Rantoul, IL].

evolution, *n.*

The six days it took God to create the universe [Melinda Lyons, Prescott, AZ].

extraordinary rendition, *n.*

Outsourcing torture [Milton Feldon, Laguna Woods, CA].

fairer, *adj.*

Regressive [Katrina vanden Heuvel, New York].

faith, *n.*

The stubborn belief that God approves of Republican moral values despite the preponderance of textual evidence to the contrary [Matthew Polly, Topeka, KS].

faith-based initiatives, *n.*

1. Trust us, have faith. [Anon].

2. Don't ask questions. [George Stuart, Tampa Bay, FL].

3. Praying to God that America can grow its way out of Bush's deficits [Anon].

4. Searching for Iraqi WMDs [John Earl, address unknown].

faith community, *n.*

1. Evangelicals, because they are saved.

2. Some token Jews and Catholics, because they are politically useful.

3. Muslims need not apply [Mathew Polly, Topeka, KS].

family values, *n.*

Heterosexuality [Michael Barry, West Medford, MA].

few bad apples, *n. phr.*

Donald Rumsfeld, Paul Wolfowitz, General Geoffrey Miller, Alberto Gonzales, George Bush; *see also* ABU GHRAIB [Robert Clawson, Acton, MA].

filibuster, *n.*

Undemocratic parliamentary trick employed by a power-crazed minority run amok [Joel Nance, Lawrence, KS].

fiscal conservative, *n.*

1. A vanishing subspecies of the Republican party [Katrina vanden Heuvel, New York, NY].

2. Going deeper into debt via military spending rather than social spending [David Kantrowitz, Olney, MD].

fiscal rectitude, *n.*

Rectal fiscitude [Alan Luchetti, Sydney, Australia].

flatus, *n.*

1. A gas generated in the stomach or bowels.

2. Something consistently confused by the president with AFFLATUS, a divine importing of knowledge or power, causing him to confuse the rumblings in his gut with the voice of God [Terence Bailey, New York, NY].

flip-flopper, *n.*

One who understands that certain issues are complex, with no black-or-white answers [Leut Phomma, Hollywood, CA].

Fox News, *fict.*

1. Faux news [Justin Rezzonico, Keene, NH].

2. White House press office in Manhattan, [Donnalyn Murphy, San Francisco, CA].

3. "We distort. You comply" [Maggie Swanson, Marion, IA].

freedom, *n.*

1. What Arabs want but can't achieve on their own without Western military intervention; it bears a striking resemblance to chaos [Matthew Polly, Topeka, KS].

2. God-given right of every American to agree with Bush and his policies [Ken Guarino, Miami, FL].

3. Ability of big business to conduct its operations without the interference of pesky political representatives of the people [Sandra Swayze, Lexington, KY].

4. F(ascist) R(epublicans) E(ncroach) E(rode) D(emocracy) O(verrule) M(ajority) [Cynthia Ambrogne-O'Toole, Scarborough, MA].

freedom fighters, *n.*

Insurgents supported by the CIA [Dan McWilliams, Santa Barbara, CA].

freedom fried, *tr. v.*

To invade Iraq [*Anon*].

free markets, *n.*

Halliburton no-bid contracts at taxpayer expense [Sean O'Brian, Chicago, IL].

free press, *n.*

1. Government propaganda materials covertly funded with a quarter of a billion dollars of taxpayer money but given out for free to the press and then broadcast without any acknowledgment of the government's role in their preparation.

2. Newspapers that obscure the truth on behalf of corporate and government interests for free [Stephen R. Shalom, NJ].

free-speech zone, *n.*

1. Pockets of the country where first-amendment rights apply, usually located out of earshot of the president [Carol Landi, Elkhart, IN].

2. The area to which those who differ from the administration are confined, should they be so audacious as to wish to exercise their right of free speech [Stephen R. Shalom, NJ].

frivolous lawsuits, *n.*

Those filed against corporations who donate heavily to the GOP [Fred Bonavita, San Antonio, TX].

girly men, *n.*

Males who do not grope women inappropriately [Nick Gill, Newton, MA].

God, *n.*

1. The Republican in chief [David Baker, Brisbane, Australia].

2. Senior presidential adviser [Martin Richard, Belgrade, MT].

God Bless America, *phrase.*

A magnet made in China, frequently located on Toyota Land Cruisers and other Japanese cars [Robert Kamper, Round Rock, TX].

G.O.P., *acronym.*

1. Greedy One Percent, the most important part of the Republican base [Richard Wales, Portland, OR].

2. "Got Ours" Party [Sheri Edwards, Knoxville, TN].

3. Greedy Opportunistic Predators [Frank and Judy Meyers, Madison, WI].

growth, *n.*

1. The justification for tax cuts for the rich.

2. What happens to the national debt when Republicans cut taxes on the rich [Matthew Polly, Topeka, KS].

gubmint, *n.*

The federal government of the United States or any of its departments, agencies, bureaucrats, dopeheads, liberal wonks, geeks, queers, coloreds, and other pinko types we don't much care for [L. J. Klass, Concord, NH].

habeas corpus, *n.*

Archaic Latin term, no longer used [Josh Wanstreet, Nutter Fort, WV].

hard work, *n.*

Tearing down the New Deal [Brian McDowell, Durham, NC].

health savings account, *n.*

1. Another tax shelter for the healthy and the wealthy [Ann Wegher, Montello, WI].

2. Investment capital for banks [Bill DiNome, Wilmington, NC].

healthy forest, *n.*

1. Forests made safe from the ravages of nature (i.e., bugs and fires) by removal to pulp mills and lumberyards [Chip Ward, UT].

2. Green lumber [Norm Conrad, Seattle, WA].

3. No Tree Left Behind [Dan McWilliams, Santa Barbara, CA].

4. Clear-cutting [Gary Schroller, Bellaire, TX].

historical interest, *n.*

A National Security memo warning of an imminent terrorist attack on the United States [Jon Rudd, Bethesda, MD].

homeland, *n.*

A term successfully used by the Germans and the Soviets in World War II, less successfully (and in the plural) by Apartheid-era South Africa, meaning neither home nor land; it has replaced both "country" and "nation" in American public speech and is seldom wielded without the companion word "security"; it is the place to which imperial forces return for R&R [Tom Engelhardt, New York, NY].

homelandism, *n.*

A neologism for love of the Homeland Security State, as in *"My Homeland, 'tis of thee, sweet security state of liberty . . ."* [Tom Engelhardt, New York, NY].

homeland security, *n.*

Synonymous with homeland insecurity [Tom Engelhardt, New York, NY].

Homeland Security Advisory System, *n.*

Color-coded program for emotional destabilization [Arlie Hochschild, Berkeley, CA].

Homeland Security Department, *n.*

The new Defense Department, known for declaring bridges yellow and the Statue of Liberty orange [Tom Engelhardt, New York, NY].

homeschooling, *n.*

An educational system where the students know more about science than the teachers [Dana Kilcrease, LaGrangeville, NY].

honesty, *n.*

Lies told in simple declarative sentences— e.g., "Freedom is on the march." [Katrina vanden Heuvel, New York, NY].

hostage, *n.*

Detainee with a ransom note the U.S. government refuses to pay [Raymond Anderson, Rantoul, IL].

House Ethics Committee, *n.*

1. Formerly, the Tom DeLay retirement commission.

2. Currently, the Tom DeLay fan club [Diane Mayr, Salem, NH].

House of Representatives, *n.*

Exclusive club, entry fee $1 to $5 million [Adam Hochschild, San Francisco, CA].

housing program, *n.*

Government expenditure for citizens in need of affordable shelter, which drains valuable funding from the war on terror [Raymond Anderson, Rantoul, IL].

humbled, *adj.*

What a Republican says right after a close election and right before he governs in an arrogant manner [Katrina vanden Heuvel, New York, NY].

humble foreign policy, *n.*

The invasion of any sovereign nation whose leadership the Republicans don't like [Matthew Polly, Topeka, KS].

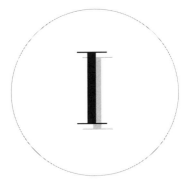

incompetence, *n.*

Requirement for promotion in the Bush administration (*see* RICE, CONDOLEEZZA; WOLFOWITZ, PAUL; BOLTON, JOHN; GONZALEZ, ALBERTO) [Terence Bailey, New York, NY].

infanticide, *n.*

Abortion [Ray Sharbutt, Moriarty, NM].

intelligence, *n.*

What Dick Cheney wants and the CIA must provide—or else (*see* IRAQ, WEAPONS OF MASS DESTRUCTION) [Tom Engelhardt, New York, NY].

international law, *n.*

1. Obsolescent principles that only apply when the administration finds it convenient [Michael Forman, Seattle, WA].

2. What other countries must abide by [Sean O'Brien, Chicago, IL].

3. An unacceptable counterweight to the "might makes right" value system [Christofer Nigro, Buffalo, NY].

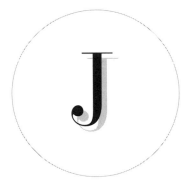

job growth, *n.*

Increased number of jobs an American has to take after losing earlier high-paying job [John E. Tarin, Arlington, VA].

journalism, *n.*

Paid political announcements; *see* PROPAGANDA [Michael Fisher, Monte Rio, CA].

journalistic integrity, *n.*

The most expensive aspect of the White House communications budget. [Jacob McCullar, Austin, TX].

junk science, *n.*

1. Any theory based on data, research, experimentation, and rigorous testing rather than on religious texts [Kaye Diefenderfer, Maitland, FL].

2. Any science that interferes with corporate profits [Bill Carson, Scottsdale, AZ].

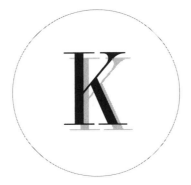

known knowns, *n.*

Things one claims one knows one knows; *see* IRAQ'S NUCLEAR PROGRAM, GOD'S WILL [Rusty Harris, Idyllwild, CA].

known unknowns, *n.*

Things one claims one knows one doesn't know; *see* ABU GHRAIB TORTURE POLICY. *Related term*: UNKNOWN UNKNOWNS, *n.* Things one doesn't know shit about; *see* PAUL WOLFOWITZ, IRAQ WAR CASUALTIES [Rusty Harris, Idyllwild, CA].

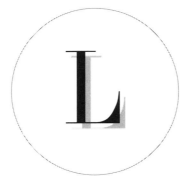

laziness, *n.*

When the poor are not working [Justin Rezzonico, Keene, OH].

leisure time, *n.*

When the wealthy are not working [Justin
Rezzonico, Keene, OH].

liberal, *adj.*

Widely used after the words "progressive,"
"radical," "left," "revolutionary," and "insur-
rectionary" were banned from the mainstream
media, having the double benefit of making
moderates seem vaguely dangerous and
making revolutionaries seem vaguely embar-
rassing and ineffectual. *Related term:* LIBERAL
MEDIA: Ted Koppel and anarchist zines
[Rebecca Solnit, San Francisco, CA].

liberal(s), *n.*

1. Followers of the Antichrist [Ann Wegher, Montello, WI].

2. Anyone who criticizes American policy, who believes in the Just War Theory, who holds an internationalist rather than stringently nationalist perspective, and who believes that America may not be the greatest nation on Earth but is part of an equitable international community [Christofer Nigro, Buffalo, NY].

libertarian, *n.*, *adj.*

Republican In Name Only; *see* RINO [Nick Gill, Newton, MA].

life, *n.*

A zygote [Daniel Warren, Chevy Chase, MD].

majority rule, *n.*

Those with the majority of the money, rule [Larry Pinkerton, Readyville, TN].

mandate, *n.*

1. The opinion expressed by about a quarter of the eligible voters.

2. The opinion reflected in an electoral-vote margin smaller than in any twentieth-century election other than 1916 and 2000.

3. The opinion expressed by the smallest popular vote margin obtained by a sitting president since 1916 [Stephen R. Shalom, NJ].

4. 51 percent [Laura Murdaugh, Naples, FL].

5. Any Republican victory [Mike Fowler, Cincinnati, OH].

6. What George Bush claims to have won after using the prospect of men dating turning into men marrying to secure victory in Ohio [Barbara DiNunzio, Mount Sinai, NY].

7. What a Republican claims to possess when only 49 percent of the voting public loathes him instead of 51 percent.

8. Having the support of five Supreme Court justices, three of whom owe their jobs to your father [Michael Thomas, Socorro, NM].

march of freedom around the world, *phr.*

John Negroponte's career [Sheila and Chalmers Johnson, San Diego, CA].

marketplace of ideas, *n.*

Buy low, sell high [Rebecca Solnit, San Francisco, CA].

market reform, *n.*

Return to robber baron capitalism [Charles Peterson, Oberlin, OH].

marriage, *n.*

The union of one man and one woman until death do they part, unless someone younger and better-looking, preferably a staffer, shows interest; *see* GINGRICH, NEWT [Raymond Anderson, Rantoul, IL].

media, *n.*

Amoral liberal elitists who should leave Republicans alone so they can complete God's work on Earth in peace and quiet behind closed doors [Matthew Polly, Topeka, KS].

Medicare Prescription Drug Bill, *n.*

No Drug Company Left Behind [George K. McHugh, Dublin, CA].

merit, *n.*

Inherited wealth [Michael Barry, West Medford, MA].

Miller, Zell, *n.*

1. The final stage of the Southern Strategy [Jan Hovden, Lawrence, KS].

2. The ghost of Lester Maddox [Chris Pedro Trakas, New York, NY].

3. The man who shot and killed Alexander Hamilton after a particularly tough interview on *Hardball* [Drew Dillon, Arlington, VA].

4. An elephant in a jackass's clothing [James Banks, Bremerton, WA].

5. Georgia politician formerly known as Zig Zag Zell [Michael Foster, Avondale Estates, GA].

6. Rabid blue dog with an elephant complex [Gary Marx, Las Vegas, NV].

modernize, *tr. v.*

To eliminate; *see* SOCIAL SECURITY [Dan McWilliams, Santa Barbara, CA].

moral values, *n.*

1. Hatred of homosexuals dressed up in Biblical language [Matthew Polly, Topeka, KS].

2. Do as we say, not as we do [Kathleen Gait, Athens, OH].

mullah, *n.*

1. (*archaic*) Religious teacher or leader, a title of respect in Islamic countries, pronounced "mull-a."

2. (*informal*) In the modern presidential vernacular, a title of disrespect (pronounced "moo-lah") in reference to Muslims deemed too fanatical to be bought off by American "moo-lah" [Nick Turse, New York, NY].

nationalism, *n.*

How foreigners love their country (when they do); a very dangerous phenomenon that can lead to extremes of passion, blindness, and xenophobia; *see* TERRORISM [Tom Engelhardt, New York, NY].

national security, *n.*

1. Of, or pertaining to, hegemonic policies designed to facilitate the increased profitability of U.S. transnational corporations.

2. Of, or pertaining to, the continued domination of world markets by U.S. corporations.

3. Deeply ambiguous term exploited by Republican officials in order to engender the jingoistic fear needed to justify the economically inspired imperialism of the

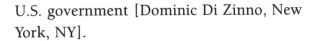

U.S. government [Dominic Di Zinno, New York, NY].

4. The ability of the president and his operatives to be secure from embarrassment, criticism, prosecution, or accountability for their actions [Raymond Anderson, Rantoul, IL].

neocons, *n.*

New con men [Mark Carberry, Denver, CO].

neoconservatives, *n.*

Nerds with Napoleonic complexes [Matthew Polly, Topeka, KS].

9/11, *n.*

Tragedy used to justify any administration policy, especially if unrelated, *see* DEFICIT, IRAQ WAR [Dan Mason, Durham, NH].

no child left behind, *riff.*

1. There are always jobs in the military [Ann Klopp, Princeton, NJ].

2. The Rapture [Samantha Hess, Cottonwood, AZ].

3. A term of political art, empowering the federal government to withhold funds from schools in poor districts, causing them to close, with the net result that the children are not left behind but instead disappear altogether [David Selby, Seattle, WA].

4. Social class divide maintenance system [Arlie Hochschild, Berkley, CA].

nonpartisan, *n.*

Member of good standing in the Federalist Society [Mark Hatch-Miller, Brooklyn, NY].

nuclear option, *n.*

1. When the commander in chief attacks senatorial prerogatives and makes the Republican moderates M.A.D.

2. An assault on the Senate rules that will leave the institution under a mushroom cloud of partisan radioactivity for years [Katrina vanden Heuvel, New York, NY].

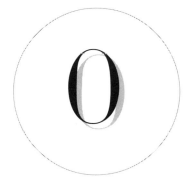

obstructionist, *n.*

Any elected representative who dares to question Bush's judicial appointments; see DASCHLE, TOM [Terry Levine, Toronto, ON, Canada].

Office of Faith-Based Initiatives, *n.*

Christian Right payoff [Michael Gendelman, Fair Haven, NJ].

oil, *n.*

1. Black gold.

2. What the Bush administration wasn't after in Iraq and isn't after in Iran; *see* DEMOCRACY [Tom Engelhardt, New York, NY].

O.I.L., *acronym.*

Operation Iraqi Liberation: coined by Dick Cheney in 2000 and accompanied by complete maps of oil fields in the Middle East with records of oil reserves, production levels, etc. [Gretchen Hecht, San Francisco, CA].

Old Testament revelations, *n.*

"God told me to strike al Qaeda and I struck, and then instructed me to strike Saddam, which I did." [George W. Bush, quoted in *Ha'aretz*].

Osama Bin Laden, *n.*

1. "I don't really think about him very much." [George W. Bush, third Kerry-Bush debate, October 2004].

2. Former ally, formerly armed by CIA; *see* BLOWBACK [Jacob McCullar, Austin, TX].

ownership society, *n.*

1. A civilization where 1 percent of the population controls 90 percent of the wealth [Michael Albert, Iscataway, NJ].

2. A culture where no one ever needs to own up to their mistakes or the consequences of their actions [Sharon Gallagher, New York, NY].

3. What the United States was before the Civil War [Sequoia Schroeder, Van Nuys, CA].

4. Texas slang for "You Own Shit" Society [Ronald Harayda, Asheville, NC].

5. Euphemism used by robber barons and their political lackeys to promote or justify

the extreme concentration of wealth into the hands of few; *see* PLUTOCRACY, COR-PORATE FEUDALISM [Ken Stump, Seattle, WA].

6. You're on your own [Josh Cohen, Evanston, IL].

7. You no longer own your national parks, your public transit, your commons, your government, your Bill of Rights, or your future, but you may purchase a Burger King franchise or some stocks with your Wal-Mart earnings [Rebecca Solnit, San Francisco, CA].

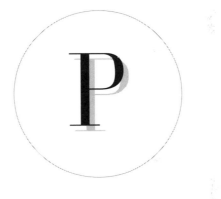

partial birth abortion, *n.*

1. Convenient wedge issue used to separate working-class social conservatives from the Democratic Party [Matthew Polly, Topeka, KS].

2. Banning of which is the first step in reversal of *Roe v. Wade* [David McNeely, Lutz, FL].

partisan attack, *n.*

Irrespective of laws, facts, or precedent, any Democrat's criticism of a Republican that would otherwise be difficult to refute [Robert Fuld, Unionville, CT].

patriot, *n.*

1. One who displays unquestioning loyalty to Republican politicians; *antonym*: Democrat [Ondi Lingenfelter, Seattle, WA].

2. One who refused to fight when it was their turn, but sends other mothers' children to war when they are in charge.

3. One who waves the flag while urging others to fight [Patty O'Grady, Fort Myers, FL].

Patriot Act, *n.*

1. The preemptive strike on American freedoms to prevent the terrorists from destroying them first.

2. The elimination of one of the reasons why they hate us [Michael Thomas, Socorro, NM].

3. Draconian legislation passed in response to 9/11 to ensure that Republicans can act patriotic while destroying the freedoms guaranteed in the Constitution [Mylo Aaron Wagner, Oceanside, CA].

4. *Extreme Makeover* edition: George Orwell's *1984* [Rory Harden, London, England].

patriotism, *n.*

How Americans love their country; a trait so positive, you can't have too much of it, and if you do, then you are a super-patriot which couldn't be better. (Foreigners cannot be patriotic; *see* NATIONALISM) [Tom Engelhardt, New York, NY].

peace, *n.*

What war is for [Rebecca Solnit, San Francisco, CA].

pension fund, *n.*

Source of money best put to use buying Texas baseball teams at inflated prices from fat cats and prodigal sons of presidents [Katrina vanden Heuvel, New York, NY].

Pentagon, *n.*

Formerly the Defense Department, but since we now have a new defense department; *see* HOMELAND SECURITY DEPARTMENT, soon to be renamed the Global Forward Deployment Department or GFDD (pronounced Gee-Fudd). Its forward-deployed headquarters will be established in a two-sided building, the Duogon, now being constructed in Bahrain out of sand imported from the beaches of Texas by Halliburton subsidiary KBR. From there, it plans to rule the known world [Tom Engelhardt, New York, NY].

personal responsibility, *n.*

1. Poor people trying to support their families on $5.75 an hour.

2. Rich people changing the tax code so their children never have to work [Chelsea Snelgrove, Atlanta, GA].

personal retirement accounts, *n.*

Chinese Communist Party loans [Katrina vanden Heuvel, New York, NY].

philosophy, *n.*

Religion [Mathew Polly, Topeka, KS].

plainspoken, *adj.*

Inability to pronounce words of more than one syllable [Jane Hawes, Emporia, KS].

political spectrum, *n.*

Moral v. Godless [Kevin Brown, Fayetteville, AR].

poor, *adj.*

1. Lazy.

2. Shiftless.

3. Lucky Ducky; see *Wall Street Journal* editorial page [Jeff Reitzes, Pleasant Hill, CA].

prayer, *n.*

Obligatory public act, best undertaken in schools and prior to football games [Michael Thomas, Socorro, NM].

presidential press conference, *n.*

1. Extremely rare phenomenon; *see* HALLEY'S COMET [Jim Nidositko, Westfield, NJ].

2. Opportunity for gay hustler to advertise his political services [Matthew Polly, Topeka, KS].

prison, *n.*

1. Rural jobs program.

2. Growth industry.

3. The only social-welfare program worthy of government funding [Michael Thomas, Socorro, NM].

pro-life, *adj.*

1. Valuing human life up until birth [Kevin Weaver, San Francisco, CA].

2. Ensuring that millions of children are uninsured [Donald Handy, Mount Clemens, MI].

progressive tax cuts, *n.*

Greater tax cuts for the rich than for the poor [Marv Vandehey, Seattle, WA].

proliferation, *n.*

1. Ally Pakistan's import-export program [Connor Livingston, Little Rock, AR].

2. From the Greek *pro* (in favor of), *life* (life), and *ration* (to be limited to); in other words, to be in favor of limiting one's life, normally to a short period of time due to the excess of weapons available worldwide, ironically also referred to as proliferation [David McCauley, Wendlebury, England].

public-opinion polls, *n.*

Progress reports for spin doctors [Michael Schwartz, address unknown].

public service, *n.*

Public serves the rich, preferably on its knees
[William Gilwood, San Dimas, CA].

quaint, *adj.*

Used to describe anything the administration would like to "qu"it doing because it "ain't" in their best interest [Aaron Andersen, Madison, WI].

ranch, *n.*

A barren, fenced wasteland, devoid of horses or livestock, in which nothing grows except scrub brush; found most frequently in West Texas [L. J. Klass, Concord, NH].

Ranch, The, *pr. n.*

The plain tract house known familiarly as the Western White House [L. J. Klass, Concord, NH].

rapture, *n.*

A probability, thanks to our commander in chief [Suzanne Saatkamp, Las Vegas, NV].

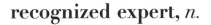

recognized expert, *n.*

Industry lobbyist [Michael Barry, West Medford, MA].

red state, *n.*

1. The blush of the belligerent [Chris Pedro Trakas, New York, NY].

2. Gray state; *see* CIVIL WAR [Anonymous Guy, 123 Sesame Street, Fantasyland, AK].

3. Reference to the facial and neck color of those who shout loudest about abortion and gay marriage; *see* MILLER, ZELL [Carol Pearson, Beech Grove, IN].

reform, *v.*

1: To end all entitlements [Herbert New, Verona, NJ].

2. To alter laws for the enrichment of Republican donors.

3. To improve corporate revenues [Douglas Falk, Prairie du Sac, WI].

4. To take from poor and give to the rich [David Katz, Tunbridge, VT].

Religious Right, *n.*

The right to do any damn thing you want because you claim God's approval [Chuck Oliver, Belford, NJ].

Republican Party, *n.*

A party that, by overturning the balance and the separation of powers, nullifying basic civil liberties, and seeking global empire, assails the foundations of the Republic [Jonathan Schell, New York, NY].

Republicenron, *n.*

Political party that believes the rights of large corporations and their chief officers are more important than ordinary citizens [Rusty Smith, Kalamazoo, MI].

rogue nation, *n.*

A country that buys its military hardware from France, China, or Russia and not from the United States [Justin Rezzonico, Keene, OH].

Rove rage, *n.*

1. Critical mass of hysterical anger harnessed by Karl Rove in 2004 over gay marriage [Durren Anderson, White Oak, TX].

2. What was unleashed on Joe Wilson's wife [Mathew Polly, Topeka, KS].

rummy, *slang n.*

1. (*archaic*) A person so drunk that he can't recall a thing.

2. (*modern*) A SECDEF so drunk on power that he refuses to remember anything [Nick Turse, New York, NY].

sacrifice, *n.*

The purchase of consumer goods on credit to improve economic growth [Tod Mohebi, Pleasanton, CA].

sanctity of marriage, *n.*

An inviolable principle, except in the case of gays and Michael Schiavo [Diane Mayr, Salem, NH].

Schiavonism, *n.*

1. When God asks Republicans to sacrifice, like Abraham, their principles about activist judges, states' rights, and the sanctity of marriage.

2. Exploitation of family tragedy for political gain [Robert Garvey, Richmond, CA].

second coming, *n.*

The reelection of George W. Bush in 2004 [Deborah Lagarde, Fort Davis, TX].

secular, *adj.*

1. Amoral.

2. God-hating [Rita Cormulley, Springfield, IL].

security, *n.*

Something to be applied to the homeland but not to the social [Rebecca Solnit, San Francisco, CA].

Senate, *n.*

Exclusive club; entry fee $10 to $30 million [Adam Hochschild, San Francisco, CA].

service economy, *n.*

"Would you like fries with that?" [Ann Gunther, Kansas City, MO].

shock and awe, *catchphr.*

A classic combination like "surf and turf"; special effects produced at missile point by the U.S. military; *see* STATE TERRORISM [Sheila and Chalmers Johnson, San Diego, CA].

simplify, *v.*

To cut the taxes of Republican donors [Katrina vanden Heuvel, New York, NY].

slam dunk, *n.*

No evidence whatsoever [Justin Rezzonico, Keene, OH].

slave, *n.*

Person without legal rights; e.g., a fetus [Matthew Polly, Topeka, KS].

slave

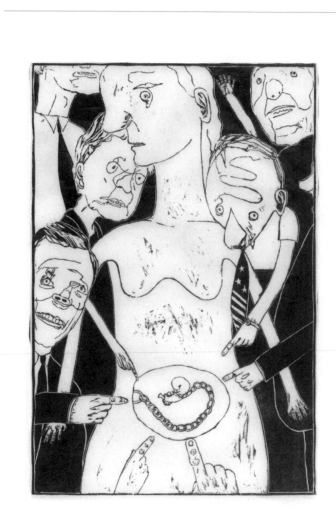

Social Security, *n.*

A good idea except for two problems: "Social" verges on socialism, and guarantees of security violate a free market [Rebecca Solnit, San Francisco, CA].

Social Security reform, *n.*

Broker security; *see* ENRON PENSION PROGRAM [Bruce Clendenin, Dallas, TX].

spreading freedom, *catchphr.*

Perpetual war [Darwin Anderson, Aurora, UT].

spreading peace, *catchphr.*

Preemptive war [Bruce Hawkins, Silver Spring, MD].

staying the course, *v.*

Saying and doing the same stupid thing over and over, regardless of the result [Suzanne Smith, Ann Arbor, MI].

stem cell, *n.*

Baby [Larry Gates, Portal, AZ].

strategic sourcing, *catchphr.*

The outsourcing of critical manufacturing industries to locations where they'll be safe from terrorist attack; see CHINA, INDIA [Bruce Reynolds, Petaluma, CA].

strict constructionist, *n.*

A judge who constructs his or her understanding of the law according to a strict conservative ideology [Vanessa deKonick, Davis, CA].

stuff happens, *phr.*

Donald Rumsfeld as master historian [Sheila and Chalmers Johnson, San Diego, CA].

support the military, *v.*

To praise Bush when he sends our young men and women off to die for a lie without proper body armor [Marc Goldberg, Vancouver, WA].

support the troops, *catchphr.*

A mandatory mantra which need no longer be mouthed since full "support" can be offered with a simple $1 investment in a magnetic yellow ribbon to affix to the back of your SUV [Nick Turse, New York, NY].

tax reform, *n.*

The shift of the tax burden from wealth to work [Dan McWilliams, Santa Barbara, CA].

tax simplification, *n.*

Way to make it simpler for large corporations exporting American jobs to get out of paying taxes [Seth Hammond, Goodwell, OK].

televangelists, *n.*

Men who possess supersensory gaydar capable of picking up homosexual agendas in cartoon characters [Raymond Rodriguez, Glen Ellyn, IL].

Ten Commandments, *n.*

1. Thou shalt not not worship God.

2. Thou shalt not display images of female breasts on network TV.

3. Thou shalt not take the name of Mary Cheney in vain.

4. Thou shalt not break the Sabbath day display of football violence for images of female breasts.

5. Thou shalt not dishonor the Daddy Party.

6. Thou shalt not kill a stem cell.

7. Thou shalt not commit sodomy.

8. Thou shalt not progressively tax the wealthy.

9. Thou shalt not file frivolous lawsuits.

10. Thou shalt not covet the Bush twins or try to get them drunk [Matthew Polly, Topeka, KS].

Texas, *state of mind.*

1. Not to be messed with.

2. The only state that still wishes it was an independent country.

3. Morally superior to Massachusetts, the birthplace of the American Revolution [L. J. Klass, Concord, NH].

theory, *n.*

Harebrained idea that has yet to be proven; *see* EVOLUTION [Justin Kodner, Princeton Junction, NJ].

Torquemada, *n.*

Former Spanish Attorney General [Martin Richard, Belgrade, MT].

tort reform, *n.*

1. Way to protect dangerous doctors from wrongfully injured patients.

2. Long-term strategy for denying Democrat candidates a source of campaign contributions [Nancy Shepherdson, Barrington, IL].

3. Preventing poor people from suing Republican campaign contributors [Gary Schroller, Bellaire, TX].

4. Corporate control of the judiciary [Michael Barry, West Medford, MA].

torture, *n.*

1. Interrogation by other means [Ann Wegher, Montello, WI].

2. Practiced only by a few bad apples [Jordan Biship, Ottawa, ON, Canada].

totalitarian communist regime, *n.*

Massachusetts [Michael Barry, West Medford, MA].

town-hall meeting, *n.*

A meeting in a hall in a town where all the participants have first been vetted for loyalty to the Bush administration [Stephen R. Shalom, NJ].

Treasury Department, *n.*

That organ of government whose purpose is to borrow sufficient funds from other countries to cover the costs of Republican spending [L.J. Klass, Concord, NH].

United Nations, *n.*

1. Bolton's buttboys [Chris Pedro Trakas, New York, NY].

2. Prime redevelopment site in an upscale East Side neighborhood with a view of the river [Rory Harden, London, England].

uniter, *n.*

Leader who brings together his followers by fomenting hatred for anyone who disagrees with him [Larry Allred, Las Cruces, NM].

vital interests, *n.*

Oil [George Price, Athens, GA].

voluntary, *adj.*

Nonexistent or ignorable. Often used in regard to industry ("the EPA established guidelines for the voluntary reduction of toxic emissions from power plants") [David Ong, CA].

voluntary compliance, *n.*

Dumping waste in rivers [Michael Barry, West Medford, MA].

voter fraud, *n.*

A significant minority turnout [Sue Bazy, Philadelphia, PA].

Wal-Mart, *n.*

The nation-state, future tense [Rebecca Solnit, San Francisco, CA].

War on Drugs, *n.*

1. Urban welfare-to-work program.

2. Prison investment program.

3. Update of the Monroe Doctrine.

4. Reason America was allied with the Taliban prior to 9/11 [Michael Thomas, Socorro, NM].

5. Million-man giveaway to the prisons-for-profit industry [Chris Pedro Trakas, New York, NY].

War on Terror, *n.*

1. An unconstitutional never-ending war on an abstract noun.

2. Best thing that ever happened to the military-industrial complex.

3. Cold War nostalgia [George Shroeder, San Francisco, CA].

Washington press corps, *n.*

Extension of White House and Pentagon press offices [Adam Hochschild, San Francisco, CA].

water, *n.*

Arsenic storage device [Joy Losee, Gainesville, GA].

wealthcare, *n.*

The trickle-down theory [Yvonne Julian-Hargrove, Fairfield, CA].

welcoming with flowers, *slang.*

Growing insurgency resulting in quagmire [Justin Rezzonico, Keene, OH].

welfare, *n.*

Evil institution that pays criminals to loaf, pop out babies, and get high [Michael Thomas, Socorro, NM].

wheelbarrow, *n.*

A retirement savings vehicle that U.S. citizens will soon use to transport the dollars needed to buy a loaf of bread when banana republic–style inflation catches up with the enormous deficits caused by unnecessary war and unwarranted tax cuts for the rich [Bill Makley, Boca Raton, FL].

wilderness, *n.*

1. Publicly owned former habitat for wildlife, often endangered, where private corporations go wild drilling for oil and gas, grazing cattle, logging, and building roads.

2. Off-road vehicle theme parks characterized by abundant stumps, oil slicks, tire tracks, flattened owls, and coughing caribou [Chip Ward, address unknown].

wildlife refuge, *n.*

An area formerly thought to be worthless but lately discovered to have valuable resources [Heath Newland, Port Washington, WI].

Willie and Horton, *n.*

Fictional gay couple Bush Jr. used to strike fear into soul of Christian Right [Barbara DiNunzio, Mount Sinai, NY].

W.M.D., *acronym*

1. Wal-Mart Deemployed. Destroys small businesspeople but leaves their stores intact [John Evans, Palmer, AK].

woman, *n.*

1. Person who can be trusted to bear a child but can't be trusted enough to decide whether or not she wishes to have the child.

2. Person who must have all decisions regarding her reproductive functions made by men whom she wouldn't want to have sex with in the first place [Denise Clay, Philadelphia, PA].

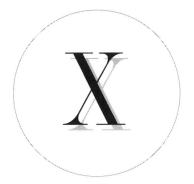

xanadu, *n.*

The Middle East after the neocons get done with it [Katrina vanden Heuvel, New York, NY].

xenophobe, *n.*

A person unduly fearful or contemptuous of foreigners—the French excepted [Katrina vanden Heuvel, New York, NY].

Young Republicans, *n.*

Drinking society for emotionally immature, sexually frustrated white boys, who believe money and Ayn Rand will solve all their problems [Katrina vanden Heuvel, New York, NY].

zealot, *n.*

A man in desperate need of a drink, *see* BUSH, GEORGE W. [Matthew Polly, Topeka, KS].

Acknowledgments

I want to thank Texas. Yes, Texas.

Texans submitted the most—and some of the sharpest—submissions. And thanks to the thousands of readers from all over the country— forty-four states in all—along with Puerto Rico and Washington, D.C., who sent me hilarious and hard-hitting definitions.

I also want to thank Kansas. Yes, Kansas. I'm one of the millions of Americans who read Tom Frank's bestseller *What's the Matter With Kansas?* and learned what's wrong with the state. Now I've learned what's right with it. His name is Matthew Polly.

A graduate of Topeka West High, Matt spent two years studying martial arts in mainland China with the famed Shaolin fighting monks. (He even represented the Temple in a challenge match. Matt won.) *American Shaolin,* Matt's account of his time in the birthplace of kung fu and Zen Buddhism, will be published in late 2006. (Watch out for his tale on movie screens near you—Fox 2000 Pictures recently acquired rights to the book.)

Matt has been a brilliant, generous, and very creative co-conspirator on this project. In these times of deceit and doublespeak, Matt's wicked and unsparing eye was invaluable. (And his definitions are some of the sharpest you'll find.)

Then there are the friends and allies who helped me take this project to another level. Tom Engelhardt is the creator and editor of the Nation Institute's Web site Tomdispatch.com. In the honorable tradition of I. F. Stone, Tom regularly informs, incites, and enlightens his growing readership.

Acknowledgments

Earlier this year, TomDispatch asked a number of its writers to contribute definitions to "A Devil's Dictionary of the Bush Era." In the spirit of positive synergy, I'm including several of the definitions gathered as part of Tom's project. I wish to thank Bill Moyers, Jonathan Schell, Rebecca Solnit, Steve Shalom, Nick Turse, Arlie Hochschild, Adam Hochschild, and Chalmers and Sheila Johnson for giving me permission to use their words. I am particularly grateful to them for their eloquent and humane work and words in these troubled times.

A few weeks into this project, I realized that while a dictionary is built on words, they could be enhanced by some subversive illustrations. As editor of *The Nation*, I've had the good fortune to work with Steve Brodner—one of America's finest illustrators and cartoonists. In the tradition of Thomas Nast, Herblock, and Ralph Steadman, Brodner has been eviscerating the mighty, the self-righteous, and the downright evil with his acid-drenched pen for three decades. Who better to turn to for help in assigning artwork for this dictionary to some of America's most creative cartoonists.

I am indebted to Ruth Baldwin of Nation Books for guiding this project—with grace, discipline, and intelligence. Thanks to Carl Bromley and John Oakes—also of Nation Books—for believing in this little book. Mark Hatch-Miller was a fastidious organizer of submissions. Mark Sorkin was the superb copyeditor of my original blogs. Michelle Risley helped with careful vetting of the manuscript in its last stage. Peter Fifield gave invaluable assistance with grammatical queries. And Peter Rothberg brought his energy and enthusiasm to the project.

Love and thanks to my husband Steve, who submitted a spicy definition. You are the straightest talking guy I know. And I'm grateful to my beloved daughter Nika who always says what she means and means what she says.

Finally, this book is dedicated to the readers of *The Nation*. Thank you for contributing your humor, heart, and head to this project to take back our language and our country.

Postscript

September 7, 2005

Dear Reader,

Dictionary of Republicanisms was completed prior to the hurricane with which I uncomfortably share the same name. Its intended purpose was to strip away the lies, deceptions, and propaganda of the right wing of the Republican Party—not because I'm under any illusion that they are the only politicians who deceive but because their lies have gutted the treasury, eroded the environment, divided our society, ruined our reputation, frayed our military, undermined our security, inspired our enemies, and overall weakened America. But then the hurricane hit, and all of this became obvious.

While New Orleans and its citizens drowned, George Bush, who is more fit for his next physical exam than he is to be president, blithely went to political events in Arizona and San Diego. While New Orleans and its citizens drowned, the President of the United States of America said, "I don't think anyone anticipated the breach of the levees." While New Orleans and its citizens drowned, FEMA Director Michael Brown said he was surprised to discover there were people in the New Orleans Convention Center. While New Orleans and its citizens drowned, Homeland Security Secretary Michael Chertoff was blaming the victims for not evacuating and test-driving the latest in Republican linguistic trickery: "Unprecedented" was the word he kept using to modify the disaster on *Meet the Press,* as if this excused the utter incompetence of the federal government in protecting the country.

As the country responds, as it always does, to the suffering of its fellow citizens with charity, kindness, and prayer, we must not forget who was in charge but asleep at the wheel when this disaster hit us. As they refuse to accept responsibility and blame everyone else, we must keep the pressure on them, because the extreme poverty that prevented tens of thousands from being able to evacuate New Orleans prior to the hurricane was not an act of God, it was the result of years of Republican policy. The failure to respond in a timely fashion as the disaster unfolded on national television was not the first time the Republican White House has mismanaged a crisis; it was the latest in a long line of failures. We simply can't afford to trust them any longer. As we drain and rebuild New Orleans, the time has come to drain the right wing's self-enriching agenda from American politics and rebuild our country into a place we can be proud of again.

—Katrina vanden Heuvel